Airbrushing for Beginners

Mastering the Fundamentals of Air Art: Your Complete Guide to Starting with Airbrush Technique

Fitzpatrick J. Thompkins

Copyright © 2024 by **Fitzpatrick J. Thompkins**

All rights reserved

No part of this publication may be reproduced, stored in a retrieval system, or transmitted, in any form or by any means, electronic, mechanical, photocopying, recording, or otherwise, without the prior written permission of the author.

The information in this ebook is true and complete to the best of our knowledge. All recommendation are made without guarantee on the part of author or publisher. The author and publisher disclaim any liability in connection with the use of this information.

Table of Contents

Introduction — 4
    What is Airbrushing? — 7
    History of Airbrushing — 9
    Benefits of Airbrushing — 11
    Overview of Airbrushing Techniques — 13

Chapter 1: Getting Started — 16
    Choosing Your Airbrush — 16
    Essential Equipment and Materials — 19
    Setting Up Your Workspace — 22
    Safety Tips for Airbrushing — 25

Chapter 2: Basic Techniques — 28
    How to Hold an Airbrush — 28
    Basic Strokes and Patterns — 31
    Using Templates and Stencils — 34
    Mixing and Matching Colors — 37
    Cleaning and Maintenance — 40

Chapter 3: Intermediate Techniques — 43
    Layering and Blending Colors — 43
    Creating Gradients and Shadows — 46
    Texturing Effects — 49
    Working with Different Surfaces — 52

Chapter 4: Advanced Techniques — 55

Realistic Portraits and Landscapes	55
Custom Designs for Vehicles and Gear	58
Using Friskets and Masks	61
Airbrushing with Metallic and Pearlescent Paints	64
Conclusion	*67*

Introduction

In the heart of downtown, nestled between a bustling café and an old bookshop, stood a quaint art supply store that Marissa frequented. She was a passionate beginner in the world of airbrushing, drawn to the vibrant swirls and intricate details that airbrushed art could produce. Yet, despite her enthusiasm, Marissa found herself struggling with the basics. That is until she discovered a book titled "Airbrushing for Beginners" tucked away on a dusty shelf in her favorite store.

The cover featured a stunning airbrushed sunset, so lifelike that Marissa felt as if she could walk right into it. Intrigued, she flipped through the pages, each chapter laid out like a step on a clear path through the misty world of airbrushing. From choosing the right airbrush to mastering advanced techniques like creating gradients and textures, the book promised to guide her through it all.

Convinced, Marissa purchased the book and set up her airbrushing station at home. As she read through the first chapter, she realized why this book was different. It wasn't just a manual; it was a mentor. The tone was friendly, the instructions clear, and the examples inspiring. It covered everything — from setting up her workspace to ensuring safety, which made Marissa feel prepared and secure.

She progressed to the projects section, eager to put her skills to the test. The book walked her through several beginner projects, starting with simple patterns and moving up to more complex designs like airbrushing a cosmic scene on a t-shirt. Each project was a building block, enhancing her confidence and skill level.

But it wasn't just the practical guidance that made the book invaluable. It was the troubleshooting section that saved many of her projects from disaster. Whenever Marissa hit a snag, like paint sputtering out of her airbrush or colors not blending smoothly, the book had a solution ready. It felt as though the author had anticipated every problem a beginner might encounter and prepared her to face it with confidence.

As weeks turned into months, Marissa's skills grew exponentially. She started sharing her creations online and received an outpouring of support and admiration from the community. Her art even caught the eye of a local café owner, who commissioned her to create a mural.

One evening, while sipping coffee next to her completed mural, Marissa reflected on her journey. She realized that "Airbrushing for Beginners" was more than just a purchase; it was an investment in her passion and a cornerstone of her artistry. The book didn't just teach her techniques; it opened doors to opportunities and sparked connections with fellow artists.

Marissa decided to write a review, hoping to assist others like her. She wrote about how the book was perfectly tailored for beginners, with its detailed explanations, step-by-step projects, and supportive guidance. She emphasized that anyone standing on the threshold of airbrushing, full of curiosity but hesitating due to uncertainty, should consider this book their gateway to mastering the art.

Through her story, Marissa not only highlighted the comprehensive nature of "Airbrushing for Beginners" but also its role as a catalyst in transforming a novice into a confident artist. It wasn't just about learning to airbrush; it was about embracing an artistic journey with a reliable guide by your side.

What is Airbrushing?

Airbrushing is a unique painting technique that uses a small, air-operated tool to spray various media, most commonly paint, by a process of nebulization. This method allows for a fine mist of paint to be applied smoothly over surfaces, creating a wide range of effects and finishes that are often difficult to achieve with traditional brushes. It's particularly popular for achieving gradients and shadows, as well as detailed graphics on a variety of surfaces, including canvas, paper, fabric, and even more unconventional substrates like automotive bodies and cakes.

The fundamental appeal of airbrushing, especially for beginners, lies in its ability to produce flawless, continuous color layers and subtle transitions in shading. This can be particularly enticing for artists and hobbyists who wish to explore new dimensions of creativity beyond the capabilities of ordinary painting techniques. The versatility of airbrushing enables not just painting but also decorating, modeling, and other artistic endeavors, making it a valuable skill for anyone interested in diverse forms of visual art.

Getting started with airbrushing requires some basic equipment, including the airbrush itself, an air source like a compressor, and suitable inks or paints. The airbrush tool comes in various types, each suited to different applications, offering control over the fineness of the spray and the viscosity of media it can handle. Learning to control the airbrush is the first step for any beginner, involving how to manipulate the flow of air and paint to achieve desired effects.

Moreover, airbrushing stands out due to its clean, even coats, which are ideal for applications requiring a high-quality finish, such as photographic retouching, nail art, and automotive painting. The technique allows for the layering of colors without the interference of brush strokes, resulting in highly professional results. For beginners, mastering airbrushing not only opens up a world of artistic possibilities but also enhances their potential in various industries, including graphic design, makeup, and custom car painting.

Aspiring airbrush artists often find that practicing this art form improves their precision and attention to detail, skills that are beneficial across many artistic disciplines. The learning process itself, from handling the equipment to applying the first layers of paint, is deeply rewarding. Through airbrushing, artists can express their creativity in ways that traditional painting methods cannot match, making it an exciting and fulfilling endeavor for beginners eager to make their mark in the world of art.

History of Airbrushing

The history of airbrushing is a fascinating journey that stretches back to the late 19th century. Originally invented by Francis Edgar Stanley in 1876, the airbrush was later perfected by his brother, Charles, and patented in 1877. The device was first developed to rapidly apply photographic retouching, which was labor-intensive when done by hand. The Stanleys' invention allowed for a fine mist of paint to be applied, which could gradually build up tones and shading much more subtly than brushwork.

As the technology evolved, so did its applications. By the early 20th century, airbrushing began to be seen as a valuable tool not just in photography but also in commercial art. The ability to produce smooth, even coats of color with soft edges made it ideal for creating advertisements and illustrations in magazines. During this period, airbrushing became synonymous with professional-grade artwork, revolutionizing how products and concepts were visually marketed to the public.

The versatility of airbrushing led to its embrace by different industries, including automotive and fashion. In the mid-20th century, airbrushing gained prominence in the customization of cars, where it was used to create intricate, eye-catching designs on vehicles. This practice highlighted the airbrush's capacity for detailed artistic expression, contributing to the rise of airbrushed art as a respected genre in its own right.

Furthermore, the fashion world took notice of airbrushing in the late 20th century, using the technique to create unique, vibrant clothing and accessories that stood out in the burgeoning world of high fashion and runway shows. This era marked a time when airbrushing became not just a tool for subtle enhancements but a medium for bold, artistic statements.

Artists and creatives have continued to innovate with airbrushing into the 21st century, incorporating digital technologies to expand its potential. The combination of traditional airbrushing techniques with digital editing has opened new avenues for multimedia art and has further integrated airbrushing into the fields of graphic design and digital illustration.

For beginners interested in airbrushing today, understanding this rich history is not only inspiring but also instrumental. It offers a perspective on how the technique has shaped visual culture, highlighting its adaptability and enduring relevance. Knowing the background can help novices appreciate the broad potential of airbrushing, from its traditional roots in delicate, manual detail work to its modern applications in diverse artistic endeavors. As new enthusiasts learn about airbrushing, they join a long lineage of artists who have pushed the boundaries of what can be achieved with a tool that sprays paint, a testament to the blend of technology and creativity.

Benefits of Airbrushing

Airbrushing offers a wide array of benefits that make it an appealing art form for beginners, allowing for versatility, efficiency, and unique aesthetic qualities that other painting methods struggle to match. One of the most notable advantages of airbrushing is the ability to achieve smooth, seamless gradients that are almost impossible to replicate with traditional brushes. This characteristic is particularly valuable for creating realistic skies, soft shadows, and gentle fades that give artwork a more life-like appearance.

The equipment's design also permits an unparalleled level of detail. Even those new to airbrushing can achieve fine lines and minute details much quicker than they might with conventional painting tools, making it ideal for projects that require precision such as miniature models, detailed graphic art, or intricate designs on various surfaces like automobiles and cakes.

Another significant advantage is the speed with which artists can work. Airbrushing allows for the quick application of paint, which not only speeds up the creation process but also aids in the fast coverage of large areas with a consistent layer of paint. This efficiency is particularly beneficial in commercial applications where time is money, such as in automotive painting or large-scale mural projects.

Furthermore, the nature of airbrushing minimizes brush marks and streaks, which can be a challenge for beginners working with traditional paint and brushes. This feature ensures a professional finish, even from those who are just starting out, boosting confidence and encouraging continued practice and experimentation.

The versatility of the airbrush also stands out as it can be used on a variety of surfaces, including textiles, walls, cars, and even cakes. This adaptability opens up numerous creative avenues for beginners, allowing them to explore different mediums and applications as their skills grow.

Lastly, airbrushing is inherently a clean art form because it requires minimal direct contact with the medium. This aspect reduces the mess typically associated with painting, making setup and cleanup much simpler. It also allows artists to switch colors quickly without the need for extensive washing and preparation between shades, promoting a fluid and spontaneous creative process.

Overall, the benefits of airbrushing make it an excellent choice for beginners eager to develop their artistic skills in a method that offers both ease of use and professional results. Whether looking to dabble in hobbies or consider professional pursuits, beginners will find that airbrushing provides a solid foundation for creative expression.

Overview of Airbrushing Techniques

Airbrushing techniques vary widely, offering a range of effects from subtle shading to vibrant, detailed artworks. Each technique provides unique results, making the practice flexible and broad. Beginners will benefit from understanding these techniques, as mastering them allows for more creativity and control in their projects.

Starting with the basics, single-action airbrushes are ideal for novices because of their simple mechanism. They spray paint when the trigger is pressed, regulating only the air flow, not the paint volume, which is set separately. This straightforward operation helps beginners focus on their hand movements and the distance between the airbrush and the target surface, key factors in achieving a consistent spray pattern.

As beginners become more comfortable, they might explore double-action airbrushes that offer greater control. With these, pressing the trigger releases air and pulling it back releases paint, allowing the artist to change the width and intensity of the paint flow dynamically during a single application. This control makes it possible to transition smoothly between thick lines and fine details without stopping to adjust the settings.

An essential technique to master is the dagger stroke, where the line starts thin, widens in the middle, and then tapers off again.

This is achieved by varying the distance of the airbrush from the surface and the speed of movement. The ability to perform this stroke well can significantly enhance the versatility of an airbrush artist, providing a foundation for more complex designs.

Stenciling is another popular technique, especially useful for beginners. It involves using pre-cut patterns to create precise shapes and motifs. This method is excellent for those who are less confident in their freehand skills but still wish to produce professional-looking designs. Stenciling also helps in layering colors and creating multicolored designs with clean, sharp edges.

Texture creation is an exciting area of airbrushing that beginners often explore early on. Techniques such as stippling, which involves applying small dots of paint to build up texture and depth, can be used to create organic effects such as fur, clouds, and foliage. Manipulating the distance and angle of the airbrush can vary the texture's coarseness, from fine to rough, offering numerous artistic possibilities.

Blending colors with an airbrush is a technique that involves overlapping colors while they are still wet, allowing them to mix on the surface to create smooth transitions. This is particularly useful for realistic portrayals of skies, skin tones, and reflective surfaces. The key to effective blending is a controlled, steady hand and a good understanding of how paints interact with each other and the surface.

As beginners progress, they often experiment with mixed media, incorporating airbrushing into projects that also involve acrylic brushes, markers, or colored pencils. This cross-disciplinary approach can open up new avenues for creativity, allowing the artist to combine the soft gradients of airbrushing with the precise lines of pen-and-ink or the rich textures of traditional brushwork.

Each technique, from basic single-action spraying to sophisticated color blending and mixed media applications, offers a step on the journey from beginner to skilled artist. With practice, these techniques can be combined and manipulated to forge individual artistic styles, making airbrushing a versatile and rewarding medium to explore.

Chapter 1: Getting Started

Choosing Your Airbrush

Choosing the right airbrush is a crucial step for beginners venturing into the world of airbrushing. The decision will significantly influence both the learning curve and the quality of your initial artworks. Understanding the different types of airbrushes, their mechanisms, and their suited applications will help ensure a smooth start and enjoyable experience.

Airbrushes come in various styles, each designed for specific purposes and offering different levels of control and detail. The three primary types are gravity feed, siphon feed, and side feed. Gravity feed airbrushes have a paint cup located on top of the airbrush. Gravity pulls the paint down into the air stream, allowing for a smoother flow and easier start. These airbrushes require less air pressure, making them ideal for fine detail work and smaller projects. They are also easier to clean and maintain, which is beneficial for beginners who are still learning about maintenance.

Siphon feed airbrushes, on the other hand, feature a paint bottle that attaches to the bottom or side of the airbrush. They are capable of holding more paint than gravity feed models, making them better suited for larger projects or for applications requiring extensive use of color. However, they typically require higher air pressure to operate and can be a bit more challenging to clean.

Side feed airbrushes offer a versatile setup, with the paint cup mounted on the side. This allows for the benefits of both gravity and siphon feed systems and provides excellent control over the paint flow. It also enables the user to work at various angles, which can be particularly useful for complex or intricate projects.

In addition to the feed type, beginners must also consider the action of the airbrush. Airbrushes can be categorized as single-action or double-action. Single-action airbrushes are easier to manage because pushing down on the trigger releases a fixed ratio of air and paint. This simplicity makes it a good choice for those who are just starting and looking for consistency without having to focus too much on controlling the airbrush.

Double-action airbrushes require the user to push down for air and pull back for paint, giving more control over the flow of paint and the width of the line. This type allows for greater precision and variability in effects, which can be beneficial as skills develop. However, it also means a steeper learning curve, as managing the two actions simultaneously can be challenging for beginners.

When choosing an airbrush, it's also important to consider the nozzle size. Nozzle sizes range from fine to large, with fine nozzles better suited for detailed work and large nozzles useful for spraying larger areas or thicker paints. Beginners might find it easier to start with a medium-sized nozzle, which offers a good balance between detail and coverage, making it versatile for various projects.

Lastly, the quality and durability of the airbrush should be taken into account. A well-made airbrush from a reputable manufacturer might cost more upfront but will generally offer better performance and longevity. This can be a wise investment, as a good quality airbrush can grow with your skills and continue to be a valuable tool as you move from beginner to advanced techniques.

For beginners, starting with a simple, versatile airbrush that balances ease of use with the ability to experiment with different techniques is key. A gravity-fed, double-action airbrush with a medium-sized nozzle often represents the best starting point, offering the flexibility to learn and grow in the art of airbrushing.

Essential Equipment and Materials

When starting in the world of airbrushing, having the right equipment and materials is crucial for both success and enjoyment of the art. The essential toolkit for a beginner comprises not only the airbrush itself but also several other key components that ensure efficient, clean, and creative work.

The centerpiece of any airbrush setup is the airbrush kit, which usually includes the airbrush and a compatible compressor. There are primarily three types of airbrushes: single-action, double-action, and trigger-style. Single-action airbrushes are the easiest to use, making them perfect for beginners. They allow for straightforward control of the air flow with a push-button mechanism. Double-action airbrushes offer more precision as they allow the user to control both air and paint flow, adjusting the width and intensity of the spray. Choosing a kit that suits your comfort level and the kind of work you intend to do is important.

Compressors are necessary to provide a consistent air supply to the airbrush. When selecting a compressor, look for one with an adjustable pressure gauge and a moisture trap. The pressure gauge allows you to control the air flow, which is crucial for different techniques and effects, while the moisture trap helps to keep water out of the paint mix, ensuring smoother application.

Another essential component is a variety of paints specifically formulated for airbrush use. These paints are thinner than regular acrylics or oils, allowing them to flow through the airbrush without clogging. It's advisable to start with primary colors along with black and white, as this allows for mixing to create various shades and hues. Additionally, investing in a good thinner or reducer is wise, as this will help maintain the correct paint consistency for optimal airbrush performance.

Proper cleaning supplies are also vital to maintain the airbrush and ensure its longevity. This includes specialized airbrush cleaner, cleaning brushes, and a cleaning pot. Regular cleaning after each use prevents paint buildup inside the airbrush, which can affect its performance and lead to malfunctions.

Airbrush-ready surfaces or substrates also play a critical role in the quality of the final artwork. Beginners might start with paper designed for airbrushing, but as skills advance, other surfaces like canvas, fabric, and even automotive exteriors can be explored. Each surface requires specific types of paint and preparation to ensure the best results.

Stencils and masking materials are useful for creating sharp edges and intricate designs. Beginners often find that using stencils helps in achieving more professional results as they build their freehand skills. Masking tape or liquid frisket can be used to cover areas of the work that require protection from overspray.

For those looking to truly understand the depth of their new craft, instructional books and DVDs can be invaluable. These resources often provide step-by-step tutorials, troubleshooting tips, and project ideas specifically geared towards new airbrush artists.

Finally, safety should not be overlooked. A well-ventilated workspace is crucial, as is a respirator mask specifically designed to filter out airborne particles. Gloves and protective eyewear are also recommended to protect skin and eyes from paint and solvent exposure.

Gathering these essential tools and materials will provide a strong foundation for any beginner eager to explore the art of airbrushing. With the right equipment, the process of learning and mastering airbrush techniques will not only be easier but also more enjoyable.

Setting Up Your Workspace

Setting up an effective workspace is a critical step for beginners in airbrushing, as it impacts both the quality of the artwork and the artist's safety. A well-organized, properly equipped space can make the learning process smoother and more enjoyable.

Firstly, choosing the right location is paramount. The workspace should be in a well-ventilated area to avoid the inhalation of fumes from paints and thinners. A room with windows that can be opened or a space with an exhaust fan is ideal. Ventilation systems or even a simple box fan in a window can help direct airflow appropriately.

The surface on which you work should be sturdy and spacious enough to accommodate your airbrush equipment and the items you'll be painting. A dedicated desk or table, resistant to solvents and easy to clean, would be most suitable. It should be of a height that allows for comfortable seating posture without straining the back or neck. A non-porous surface is preferable, as it won't absorb materials and can be easily wiped down after each session.

Lighting is another crucial aspect. Good lighting not only helps in achieving precise effects but also reduces eye strain. Natural light is best, but if that's not sufficient, adding bright, direct artificial lights can enhance visibility. LED lamps or daylight bulbs provide a clean, clear light that closely mimics natural sunlight.

Organizing your tools and materials efficiently can save time and reduce frustration. A shelf or a set of drawers near your work table can store airbrushes, paints, reducers, cleaning supplies, and stencils. Keeping these items within easy reach but neatly arranged prevents accidents and spills. A holder or rack specifically for airbrushes protects the equipment from damage and keeps them handy.

Protective gear is an important part of your workspace setup. Gloves, masks, and even goggles should be considered, especially when using types of paint that emit strong fumes or could cause irritation. An apron or old clothes are also advisable to protect your garments from paint splatters.

Considering the potential mess, having a cleaning station within your workspace is beneficial. This could include a wash bin, rags, paper towels, and cleaning solutions designated for airbrush equipment. Routine cleaning not only prolongs the life of your airbrush but also ensures consistent performance.

Finally, setting up an inspirational and motivational environment can foster creativity. Decorate your workspace with art that inspires you, be it prints of famous paintings or works by contemporary artists you admire. A comfortable, inviting atmosphere can make the workspace a place where you look forward to spending time and creating art.

A well-planned workspace not only facilitates efficient learning and practicing of airbrush techniques but also ensures safety and hygiene, making the art-making process a thoroughly enjoyable experience.

Safety Tips for Airbrushing

When getting started with airbrushing, prioritizing safety is crucial. The process involves not only skill and creativity but also the use of equipment and materials that can pose health risks if not handled properly. Being aware of the potential hazards and knowing how to mitigate them ensures a safer airbrushing experience, especially for beginners.

One of the primary safety concerns is the inhalation of paint particles and solvent fumes. Airbrush paints, particularly those that are solvent-based, can emit harmful vapors that may cause respiratory issues, dizziness, or other health problems over time. To protect against this, working in a well-ventilated area is essential. An airbrushing space should ideally have cross-ventilation, utilizing fans and open windows, or better yet, be equipped with a professional-grade ventilation system that directly removes fumes from the work environment.

In addition to ventilation, wearing a respiratory mask is a must. A high-quality mask designed to filter out particulates and fumes provides an additional layer of protection. It's important that the mask fits well and is specific to the type of materials used; for example, masks rated for organic vapors are suited for solvent-based paints.

Protective clothing also plays a role in airbrushing safety. Wearing long sleeves, gloves, and safety goggles helps prevent skin and eye contact with paint and solvents, which can be irritating or harmful depending on the chemicals involved. Nitrile gloves are preferred as they offer resistance to many chemicals and do not react with the solvents typically found in airbrush paints.

Another aspect of airbrush safety involves the care and maintenance of the equipment itself. Airbrushes and compressors must be properly maintained to prevent malfunction or accidents. This includes regular cleaning of the airbrush to prevent clogging and build-up of paint, which not only affects performance but could lead to unexpected spraying that might expose the user to direct contact with harmful substances. Compressors, particularly those that use oil, should be checked for signs of oil leakage and to ensure they are operating within safe temperature ranges.

Handling and storage of materials are also critical. Paints, thinners, and cleaners should be stored in a cool, dry place away from direct sunlight and heat sources to prevent degradation or spontaneous combustion. Containers should be tightly sealed to avoid spills and minimize vapor release into the work area.

Moreover, understanding the materials used is vital for safety. This means reading and adhering to the manufacturer's instructions on all products and being aware of the specific hazards associated with different types of paint and solvent. Material Safety Data Sheets (MSDS) for each product provide detailed information on handling, toxicity, and first aid measures and should be readily accessible in the work area.

Lastly, establishing good routine practices contributes significantly to safety. This includes keeping the workspace clean and organized to avoid accidents like tripping over equipment or knocking over containers of paint. Regular breaks are important, too, to reduce prolonged exposure to potential toxins and to prevent physical strain from staying in one position for too long.

By addressing these safety aspects, beginners can enjoy learning and experimenting with airbrushing while minimizing risks, making their artistic exploration both productive and secure.

Chapter 2: Basic Techniques

How to Hold an Airbrush

Holding an airbrush correctly is fundamental for any beginner, as it affects the control and final outcome of your artwork. Proper grip and posture are essential to achieving the precision and stability needed for effective airbrushing.

The most common way to hold an airbrush is similar to how one might hold a pen or pencil, which is familiar and generally comfortable. This method provides a good balance between control and comfort, allowing for fine detail work and prolonged use without excessive hand fatigue. When gripping the airbrush, place your index finger on the trigger, allowing for easy control of the air and paint flow. Your thumb and middle finger should support the body of the airbrush from underneath.

The airbrush should rest lightly in your hand, not gripped too tightly. A relaxed grip aids in smoother movement, reducing hand tremors that can lead to uneven lines or splotches. Precision in airbrushing comes not from force, but from gentle, controlled movements. Your wrist should remain flexible, as stiff movements can restrict the range of motion necessary for creating fluid, dynamic strokes.

Body posture also plays a crucial role in how you hold and maneuver the airbrush. Ideally, you should sit or stand straight, maintaining a comfortable stance that allows you to move your arm freely from the shoulder. This posture helps in maintaining steady pressure and movement, which is particularly important when working on larger pieces or surfaces. Your painting surface should be at a height where your arm can rest comfortably without having to reach or bend awkwardly, as maintaining a natural alignment reduces strain and improves control.

When airbrushing, the distance between the nozzle and the surface is critical. Typically, holding the airbrush between two to six inches away from the target surface is recommended for most applications. However, this can vary based on the type of effect you are trying to achieve. For broader coverage, increase the distance, and for finer details, decrease it. Keeping the airbrush perpendicular to the surface as much as possible ensures an even application and reduces the risk of paint running or pooling.

As you become more experienced, you might find that adjusting your grip slightly can help with specific techniques. For example, shifting the airbrush to a more pen-like grip, using your index and middle fingers on top and your thumb underneath, can offer more detailed control for intricate work. Alternatively, some artists prefer to use their thumb on the trigger and their fingers underneath the body for a sturdier hold during longer sessions or when applying larger areas of color.

Practice is key in mastering how to hold an airbrush. Spending time experimenting with different grips, distances, and movements will not only improve your skill but also help you develop a style and preference that feels most natural to you. As with any artistic tool, comfort and control are paramount, and finding the right balance is a personal journey that evolves with experience.

Basic Strokes and Patterns

In the realm of airbrushing, mastering basic strokes and patterns is crucial for beginners to establish a strong foundation in this art form. These fundamental techniques serve as the building blocks for more complex and detailed artwork. Understanding and practicing these basics can significantly enhance an artist's precision and ability to create a variety of effects.

One of the first techniques beginners learn is how to control the basic airbrush stroke. This involves operating the airbrush to produce a consistent, even line. The key is to maintain a steady hand and an even distance from the surface, typically about six to eight inches. This distance helps ensure the paint is atomized properly before it hits the surface, which is crucial for a smooth application. Artists are encouraged to practice moving the airbrush at a constant speed to achieve uniform coverage, a skill essential for both detailed work and larger, more expansive projects.

Dot making is another fundamental skill. Creating dots requires a precise control of the air trigger. A quick tap can make a small dot, while holding the trigger down a bit longer produces larger dots. The size and spread of the dot are controlled by the airbrush's distance from the surface—the closer the nozzle, the smaller and more concentrated the dot. Practicing dot creation helps artists develop their hand stability and control over the airbrush's paint flow.

Lines are a natural progression from dots. Line work with an airbrush can range from very thin to thick by adjusting the distance from the canvas and the paint flow. Beginners should practice making lines by starting with the airbrush further away from the surface and moving it closer gradually. This movement allows the line to start thin, widen, and then narrow again. Mastery of line work is crucial for creating sharp edges, precise borders, and various textures in more complex compositions.

Additionally, the dagger stroke is an important basic technique. This stroke begins with a light spray that broadens and then ends sharply as the artist pulls the airbrush away while decreasing the paint flow. Dagger strokes are essential for creating leaves, feathers, and various tapering shapes that are common in more intricate designs.

For patterns, practicing simple geometric shapes like circles, squares, and triangles is beneficial. These shapes teach control and precision and are often used as components in larger designs. A circle, for example, can be challenging as it requires the artist to move the airbrush in a smooth, steady circular motion to maintain an even line width and circular shape.

Shading and gradients are also fundamental patterns that involve varying the paint's opacity to create depth or transition between colors. Beginners should practice by gradually layering the paint, starting with a very light application and slowly increasing the density of the color to achieve a smooth gradient. This technique is particularly useful in creating realistic images and adding three-dimensional effects to flat surfaces.

Each basic stroke and pattern practice builds an artist's confidence and capability with an airbrush. Through repetitive practice of these techniques, beginners can start to explore more complex designs and begin to develop their unique artistic style. These basic skills are the cornerstone of effective airbrushing, enabling artists to produce artworks with depth, precision, and creativity.

Using Templates and Stencils

Using templates and stencils is a fundamental technique in airbrushing, especially useful for beginners who are developing their skills. This approach not only ensures clean, precise lines and shapes but also helps artists create complex designs more efficiently. Stencils can be bought pre-made or custom designed, offering limitless possibilities for creativity.

Templates and stencils work by acting as masks that cover parts of the surface, only allowing paint to pass through designated open areas. This method is perfect for producing sharp edges and detailed patterns that might be difficult to achieve freehand when you're still getting comfortable with the airbrush. For beginners, this technique is an excellent way to get accustomed to the airbrush's function and behavior while also guaranteeing satisfying results with their early projects.

To begin using templates and stencils, the artist first secures them onto the work surface. It's important to affix them firmly to prevent any paint from seeping underneath. This can be done using low-tack adhesive sprays or masking tape, which hold the stencil in place but won't damage the underlying surface when removed. Ensuring that every edge of the stencil adheres closely to the surface is key to achieving clean lines.

The type of material used for the stencil also affects the outcome. Materials range from paper and cardstock to more durable options like Mylar or acetate. While paper stencils are disposable and suitable for one or a few uses, Mylar stencils are reusable and resistant to the solvents in airbrush paint, making them a more economical choice for designs that will be used repeatedly.

When applying paint with a stencil, the airbrush should be held at a 90-degree angle to the surface. This straight-on approach minimizes the risk of paint blowing under the stencil edges. The distance between the airbrush and the surface also plays a critical role; too close, and the paint may pool or cause bleed-under, too far, and the spray might become too diffuse, softening the edges. A consistent medium distance usually provides the best results.

Controlling the airbrush's pressure is crucial. Lower pressure is often better when working with stencils to help control the paint flow and reduce the chances of the paint seeping beneath the stencil edges. It's beneficial to practice on scrap material to get a feel for the right pressure settings before applying paint to the actual project.

Another technique to enhance stencil use is the 'back and forth' motion. Instead of spraying directly at the open areas, the artist moves the airbrush in a light, sweeping motion across the stencil. This technique helps distribute the paint evenly and prevents excessive buildup in any one area.

Once the painting is complete, removing the stencil carefully is essential to avoid smudging the wet paint. It should be lifted away from one corner, pulling up and away from the paint to leave a crisp design.

For intricate designs involving multiple colors or layers, artists can use multiple stencils, layering them in sequence to build up the final image. This requires precise alignment and timing—allowing each layer to dry sufficiently before applying the next—to avoid blending unwanted colors or disturbing the underlying layers.

Cleaning and maintaining stencils is also a part of the process. For paper stencils, minimal cleaning is possible, but plastic or Mylar stencils should be cleaned with appropriate solvents after each use to remove any residual paint. Proper care extends the life of these tools, ensuring sharp edges and precise shapes for future projects.

Overall, using templates and stencils is an excellent way for beginners to produce professional-looking results while still learning the finer points of airbrush technique. This method not only enhances the precision of their work but also boosts confidence as they see their capabilities grow with each project.

Mixing and Matching Colors

Mixing and matching colors in airbrushing is both an essential skill and an art form, crucial for beginners to grasp in order to create visually appealing and dynamic artworks. Understanding how to blend and combine colors effectively can elevate an airbrush artist's work from simple monochrome designs to complex and nuanced creations.

The first step in mastering color mixing with an airbrush is understanding the color wheel. The color wheel is a visual representation of colors arranged according to their chromatic relationship. Primary colors—red, blue, and yellow—cannot be made from other colors. Secondary colors—green, orange, and purple—are created by mixing two primary colors. Tertiary colors result from mixing primary and secondary colors. This basic knowledge helps in predicting the results of color mixing.

When starting with airbrushing, it's practical to mix colors outside the airbrush in a small cup or palette, using airbrush medium to thin the paint if necessary. This approach provides more control over the consistency and hue of the color before it is loaded into the airbrush. When mixing colors, it's essential to start with lighter colors and gradually add darker colors. This method is preferred because it's easier to darken a light color than to lighten a dark one.

One common technique for color mixing in airbrushing is the 'gradual blend,' where two colors are sprayed side by side on the artwork and then blended where they meet. This requires a steady hand and a fine balance in the airbrush's pressure to avoid harsh lines and ensure a smooth gradient. Practicing this technique can help artists learn how to control their airbrush and develop a feel for how different colors interact when sprayed closely together.

Color matching is another critical aspect, especially when working on larger pieces that require consistent coloration across different working sessions or when correcting mistakes. To match colors accurately, keep detailed records of the color mixes used, including the ratios and specific paints. This practice can save time and frustration when continuity in color is needed.

It's also useful for beginners to experiment with adding small amounts of complementary colors to achieve more vibrant and rich tones. Complementary colors are directly opposite each other on the color wheel, such as blue and orange or red and green. This technique can help in toning down overly bright colors or adding depth to a paint mix.

Temperature and value shifts are subtle yet impactful ways to add dimension to your work. Colors can have warm or cool undertones, and shifting these can affect the mood and spatial perception of an artwork. Lighter values (tints) can be made by adding white, while darker values (shades) can be achieved by adding black or a complementary color for a richer depth.

For beginners, it's crucial to practice these techniques on a test paper before applying them to the final piece. This practice not only builds skill but also helps in understanding how different colors and materials behave under various conditions. Over time, this experimentation leads to a more intuitive sense of color, allowing artists to make quick and effective color decisions during their creative process.

Ultimately, the ability to mix and match colors proficiently opens up endless possibilities in the realm of airbrush art, enabling the artist to convey a broader range of expressions and themes within their work.

Cleaning and Maintenance

Maintaining and cleaning an airbrush is crucial for ensuring its longevity and performance, especially for beginners who might not yet be familiar with the nuances of their equipment. Proper cleaning prevents paint buildup and clogging, which are common issues that can affect the airbrush's functionality and the quality of the artwork.

The process of cleaning an airbrush starts immediately after use. Begin by flushing out the remaining paint from the airbrush with a suitable cleaner; this could be water for water-based paints or a solvent for oil-based or enamel paints. Simply pour the cleaner into the cup where the paint was loaded, and spray it through the airbrush until it runs clear. This initial step helps to remove the majority of the residual paint.

Once the flushing is complete, it's important to disassemble the airbrush for a more thorough cleaning. This involves removing the needle, nozzle, and other removable parts. Each component should be handled with care, as they are delicate and can be damaged easily. Using specialized airbrush cleaning brushes and a soft cloth, gently clean each part. For the needle and nozzle, special attention is needed; even a small amount of dried paint can impede the airflow and disrupt the paint spray pattern. Needle tools are available to help clear blockages in the nozzle, but they must be used with caution to avoid bending or breaking the needle.

Reassembly should be done carefully to ensure that all parts are aligned correctly and securely. After reassembling, it's wise to perform a test spray with cleaner or water to ensure that the airbrush functions smoothly. If there's any splattering or uneven spray, it may indicate that there's still some obstruction or that the components aren't assembled properly.

Routine maintenance should also include checking the tightness of the nozzle and needle cap and ensuring that the trigger and other moving parts operate smoothly. A drop of lubricant designed specifically for airbrushes can be applied to the moving parts if they begin to feel sticky or stiff. This not only keeps the action smooth but also protects the airbrush from wear and corrosion.

For those who use their airbrush frequently, a deep clean might be necessary periodically. This involves soaking the metal parts in a cleaning solution to dissolve any stubborn paint deposits. However, care should be taken to avoid soaking parts like O-rings and rubber gaskets, as some solvents can cause these to deteriorate.

Storing the airbrush properly is another aspect of maintenance that can extend its life. After cleaning, the airbrush should be stored in a dry place and, if possible, left with the needle and nozzle protected. Some artists choose to store their airbrushes in a case or holder to avoid accidental drops or bumps.

Regular maintenance not only keeps the airbrush in optimal working condition but also saves time and frustration during painting sessions. Beginners will find that taking good care of their airbrush greatly enhances their overall experience and satisfaction with their artistic projects.

Chapter 3: Intermediate Techniques

Layering and Blending Colors

Layering and blending colors are intermediate airbrushing techniques that can significantly enhance the depth and realism of an artwork. For beginners ready to expand their skills, mastering these methods can be a game changer, allowing for more dynamic and intricate designs.

Layering colors with an airbrush is about applying multiple coats of paint, one over the other, to build up a final image. This technique is not just about covering one color with another; it involves strategic planning of which colors to use, in which order, and how opaque each layer should be. A foundational understanding of how different colors interact when layered is crucial. Transparent layers work best for this technique as they allow the colors underneath to show through, creating a rich, multidimensional effect.

The process begins by applying a base color, typically a lighter shade. Once the base is dry, subsequent layers are applied. The key is to gradually darken the shades with each pass. For instance, when painting a sunset, a painter might start with a light yellow, add layers of orange, and finally top with a deep red or purple at the horizon. Each layer needs to be thoroughly dried before the next is applied to prevent colors from bleeding into each other unless blending is intended.

Blending, on the other hand, is the technique of smoothing the transitions between colors. This can be done wet-on-wet, where colors are applied while the previous layers are still slightly tacky, allowing the colors to mix on the canvas. Alternatively, colors can be blended dry by using a very light touch with a second layer of paint, allowing the bottom color to influence the top layer subtly.

To achieve smooth blends, air pressure, paint viscosity, and distance from the canvas play critical roles. Lower air pressure helps in spraying a finer mist of paint, which is essential for subtle color changes. Thinning the paint can also aid in smoother blending, as thinner paint spreads more easily. Keeping the airbrush at a consistent distance from the surface ensures an even application of paint, which is vital for uniform gradients.

One popular blending technique in airbrushing is the 'back and forth fade,' where the artist moves the airbrush back and forth across a boundary between two colors, gradually merging them into one another. This motion, combined with the controlled release of paint, creates a seamless gradient. Another technique involves 'dusting,' where a very light layer of paint is sprayed over an area to subtly shift its hue or value.

Practicing these techniques on scrap material or in a sketchbook can be incredibly beneficial. It allows beginners to experiment with different pressures, distances, and paint mixtures without the pressure of ruining a project. Over time, these practices help in developing a more intuitive sense for how much paint to apply and how to manipulate the airbrush to achieve desired effects.

Overall, layering and blending are techniques that elevate the art of airbrushing. They provide artists with the tools to create more vibrant, realistic, and visually interesting pieces. As beginners master these skills, they will find themselves able to tackle more complex projects with confidence and creativity.

Creating Gradients and Shadows

Creating gradients and shadows with an airbrush is an essential skill for artists looking to add dimension and realism to their work. This technique allows for the seamless blending of colors and the creation of depth, transforming flat images into dynamic visuals. For beginners who have mastered basic airbrushing skills, learning how to effectively produce gradients and shadows is a crucial next step in their artistic development.

Gradients, or smooth transitions between colors, are foundational in airbrushing. They can mimic natural lighting effects, convey a sense of volume, and enhance the overall composition of a piece. To create a gradient, the artist starts by selecting two or more colors that blend well together. Typically, one would start with the lighter color, spraying it at a low air pressure for more control. The key is to apply the paint in thin, even layers, gradually building up the intensity at the desired starting point of the gradient.

Once the base layer is down, the artist then switches to the darker color. This color is applied starting from where the gradient should be darkest, slowly working back towards the lighter area. The overlap of the two colors should be handled with a very light hand, allowing the colors to merge naturally. By adjusting the distance of the airbrush from the surface, the artist can control the softness of the gradient; closer distances result in a more concentrated color, while pulling the airbrush further away spreads the paint over a wider area, softening the transition.

Shadows, on the other hand, are about creating the illusion of light and depth. Shadows are not simply a darker shade of the base color; they often incorporate complementary colors to achieve a more realistic effect. For instance, shadows on yellow objects may contain some purple to enhance the depth perception. When creating shadows, it's crucial to consider the light source in the artwork, as this will dictate where the darkest tones should be placed.

To apply shadows, the artist begins by lightly sketching out where the shadows will fall using a very diluted version of the shadow color. This initial sketch acts as a guide and prevents common mistakes like overly harsh or misplaced shadows. After laying down this guide, the artist uses the airbrush to build up the shadow, increasing the paint's opacity toward the area farthest from the light source. This technique requires a steady hand and a good sense of how light interacts with objects.

For both gradients and shadows, an effective technique is to continuously adjust the airbrush's air pressure. Lower pressures are great for fine, detailed work and for softening the edges of a shadow or gradient, while higher pressures can cover larger areas more quickly. Furthermore, practicing control over the trigger of

47

the airbrush is vital as it directly affects the flow of paint and the resultant smoothness of the gradient or depth of the shadows.

Lastly, patience is essential when creating gradients and shadows. Multiple light layers are preferable to a few heavy ones, as they offer more control and produce a more professional finish. Overworking a single area too quickly can lead to drips or uneven layers, which can disrupt the smooth aesthetic required for realistic gradients and shadows.

For beginners looking to advance their airbrushing skills, mastering the creation of gradients and shadows not only improves their technique but also expands their ability to express depth and emotion in their art.

Texturing Effects

Texturing effects in airbrushing offer artists the ability to add dimension, depth, and realism to their work, transforming flat images into vivid, tactile surfaces. For beginners transitioning to intermediate techniques, learning to create texture with an airbrush is a vital skill that broadens the scope of their projects and introduces new challenges that enhance their proficiency.

Creating texture with an airbrush involves manipulating paint flow, air pressure, and the distance between the airbrush and the surface to achieve various effects. One common method is the use of stippling, where the artist sprays small dots onto the surface. By varying the size of the dots and how densely they are applied, you can create the illusion of different textures. This is particularly effective for replicating surfaces like sand, gravel, or even skin pores, depending on the fineness of the spray.

Another technique is called erasing or back spraying, where artists use an airbrush to apply a layer of paint and then partially remove it with a tool like an eraser or a rag while it's still wet. This can produce a worn, distressed look ideal for aging effects or adding character to surfaces like metal or wood. This method requires a delicate touch to ensure that the underlying layers are not completely obscured, maintaining a balance between the old and new layers of paint.

For those looking to achieve more complex textures, masking techniques can be employed. Using frisket film or masking tape, artists can cover parts of their work and spray over the top. Removing the mask then reveals the untouched area underneath, creating sharp edges that contrast with the textured regions. This is highly effective for mechanical or geometric designs, where precision is key. Masking can also be used in layers to build up complex textures gradually, adding a rich depth to the artwork.

Creating textures with additives is another approach. Mixing additives like sand, textile mediums, or even salt into the paint before spraying can add a tactile quality to the paint itself. These materials interact with the surface in unique ways, giving the final piece a distinctive feel that cannot be achieved with paint alone. However, this method requires testing and experimentation to see how different additives affect the flow of paint through the airbrush.

Splattering is a more spontaneous technique that creates lively, random textures. This can be done by altering the air pressure or by manually flicking paint onto the canvas using an old brush or a toothbrush. The splattered paint creates a speckled effect that is ideal for portraying dirt, stars in a night sky, or an abstract background. The unpredictability of splattering means each piece is unique, adding an element of surprise to the creative process.

Using a dry brush technique over airbrushed layers can also produce interesting textures. By lightly dragging a dry brush with minimal paint over an area that has been airbrushed, artists can create highlights and shadows that mimic the roughness or bumpiness of surfaces like bark, stone, or fabric.

Intermediate artists often combine several of these techniques to create complex textures. For example, one might start with a stippled background, add layered masking for geometric designs, and finish with splattering for a final touch of randomness. Each layer contributes to the overall depth and realism of the piece, allowing the artist to develop a nuanced and textured surface that draws viewers into the artwork.

Mastering texturing effects with an airbrush not only enhances the visual appeal of artworks but also gives artists the tools to express their creative visions more fully. This exploration of texture opens up new avenues for artistic expression and sets the foundation for advanced airbrushing techniques.

Working with Different Surfaces

Working with different surfaces is an exciting chapter in the airbrushing journey, especially for those who have moved past the basics and are looking to expand their skills and artistic reach. Different surfaces react uniquely to airbrush paint, affecting everything from texture and adhesion to the final visual effects. Understanding these interactions can greatly enhance the versatility and impact of an artist's work.

Canvas is a popular choice for airbrush artists, primarily because of its adaptability and forgiving nature. When airbrushing on canvas, the paint layers smoothly, allowing for fine gradients and subtle color shifts that are ideal for realistic artworks. Pre-priming the canvas with a suitable gesso can improve paint adherence and longevity, ensuring the artwork remains vibrant and durable over time.

Airbrushing on fabric is another intriguing possibility, often used in custom apparel and textile design. Specialized fabric paints are necessary for this medium to ensure that the colors bond well with the fibers and remain flexible without cracking when the fabric is worn or washed. Artists typically stretch the fabric on a frame to keep it taut while working, and heat-setting the paint afterward ensures the design's durability. Techniques vary depending on the fabric's weave; tightly woven fabrics like silk allow for sharp, detailed work, while coarser fabrics like cotton are better for bold, graphic designs.

Automotive airbrushing brings its own set of challenges and rewards. Cars, motorcycles, and helmets are common canvases in this niche. Working on these surfaces requires paints that can adhere to metal and withstand the elements. Automotive urethane paints are a preferred choice because of their durability and vibrant colors. Surface preparation involves thorough cleaning, sanding, and often applying a primer to ensure the paint sticks well and stands up to sunlight and weathering.

Plastic and metal models are popular among hobbyists who use airbrushing to add intricate details and weathering effects that mimic real-life textures. These surfaces require an acrylic or enamel paint that adheres well to smooth surfaces. Priming is crucial; a good primer provides a base that ensures the paint layers up evenly without beading or running. Additionally, sealing the finished piece with a clear coat can protect the paint job against handling and display elements.

For those interested in culinary arts, airbrushing on cakes and other edibles introduces a unique medium. Edible paints must be used, and the surface is often irregular and absorbent. Artists typically work on a fondant or a smooth icing base, which can hold colors well. The challenge here is to apply the paint quickly and evenly before the surface becomes too moist and begins to degrade the artwork.

Glass and ceramics offer a slick, non-porous surface that can be difficult to paint. Specialized glass or ceramic paints that can fuse to the surface under high temperatures (such as in a kiln) are necessary for long-lasting results. Techniques include masking areas to create designs and using alcohol to blend and set the paint before firing.

Wood is another versatile surface for airbrushing, favored for its natural texture and warmth. Preparing wood usually involves sanding it smooth and applying a sealant to prevent the paint from soaking into the grain unevenly. Artists can achieve stunning effects by letting some of the natural grain show through semi-transparent layers or by using the wood's texture as part of the artwork's overall design.

Exploring these different surfaces not only broadens the scope of projects an airbrush artist can undertake but also deepens their understanding of how materials interact with their medium. Mastery over various surfaces allows artists to select the best base for their designs, tailoring their approach to each project for optimal results. Each surface offers unique challenges and possibilities, making the exploration of airbrushing on different bases an enriching progression for any artist.

Chapter 4: Advanced Techniques

Realistic Portraits and Landscapes

Creating realistic portraits and landscapes with an airbrush requires a blend of technique, precision, and artistic interpretation. For beginners moving into more advanced airbrushing, mastering these subjects can be both challenging and immensely rewarding. The journey to proficiency begins with an understanding of the foundational skills and progresses to the nuances that bring realism to life.

Realistic portraits with an airbrush demand a keen eye for detail and a deep understanding of human anatomy. Beginners should start by studying facial features and proportions, often using reference photos to guide their work. The goal is to capture not just the likeness but also the essence of the subject. This involves careful observation of how light and shadow play across the face, defining features and expressions. Using a double-action airbrush is crucial here as it allows the artist to control the paint flow and air pressure precisely, enabling them to build up layers of color gradually. The process typically starts with a neutral base tone, upon which darker shadows and lighter highlights are added. These layers must be blended seamlessly, a technique that might require a slower, more patient approach but results in a more lifelike representation.

For the finer details such as the eyes, which are often considered the windows to the soul, a very fine nozzle and minimal paint flow are essential. The eyes can bring a portrait to life or render it lifeless, so special attention to the reflection highlights, the gradation of the iris, and the sharpness of the eyelashes can make a significant difference. Similarly, the lips and hair require multiple layers of color to add depth and texture, with translucent over-sprays to create natural variations found in real human features.

Transitioning to landscapes, the airbrush is an ideal tool for capturing the vastness and detail of natural scenes. Here, the focus shifts to understanding perspective and the interaction of elements at different distances. Beginners should practice techniques like aerial perspective, which involves painting more distant elements with less detail and lighter tones to simulate atmospheric haze. The airbrush naturally creates soft edges and subtle color transitions, perfect for the sky, distant mountains, or reflections in water.

Landscapes often require a broader color palette and the ability to blend these colors smoothly across large canvases. Techniques like color layering and underpainting are beneficial. Underpainting involves creating a monochrome version of the scene to establish values and depth before color is applied. This method helps in managing the complexity of the scene and ensures that the final colors pop with the right intensity and hue.

Texture in landscapes is achieved through various airbrushing techniques such as stippling for foliage or sponge techniques for irregular patterns like rocks or tree bark. Each texture requires a different approach to the angle and distance of the airbrush from the canvas, as well as the viscosity of the paint used. Experimentation and practice are crucial, as the behavior of paint can change with environmental factors like humidity and temperature, affecting the final outcome.

Advanced airbrush artists often use a combination of freehand techniques and the use of friskets or masks to protect certain areas and create sharp contrasts or hard lines where needed, such as the horizon line in a landscape or the sharp contrasts in lighting on a portrait.

As beginners advance in their skills, the complexity of their projects will naturally increase. Realistic portraits and landscapes are ambitious projects that can serve as significant milestones in an artist's airbrushing journey. Each piece, with its challenges and intricacies, not only enhances the artist's technical skills but also deepens their appreciation of the visual world.

Custom Designs for Vehicles and Gear

Airbrushing custom designs onto vehicles and gear represents an exciting leap from beginner techniques to more advanced applications of airbrush art. This niche allows artists to transform everyday objects and vehicles into personalized statements or works of art. The process combines technical skill with creative vision, pushing the boundaries of what can be achieved with an airbrush.

Custom vehicle airbrushing often begins with a concept or a request from a client. The artist must consider the contours and color of the vehicle to ensure the design complements its form. This might involve sketching the design on paper or using digital software to visualize how the artwork will wrap around three-dimensional surfaces. Once the design is finalized, the surface preparation begins, which is crucial for ensuring the longevity and vibrancy of the airbrushed art.

Surface preparation involves cleaning, sanding, and sometimes priming the surface of the vehicle to ensure that the paint adheres well and lasts long. Special automotive airbrush paints are used because of their durability and range of colors. These paints must be compatible with automotive topcoats to protect the finished art from weather and wear.

The airbrushing process itself requires precision and control. Artists need to adjust their technique based on the design's complexity and the effects they wish to achieve. For example, shading and gradients might be used to give the illusion of depth and motion, while stencils can be employed for precise, repeatable patterns. Techniques like masking and layering are also common, allowing for the creation of intricate, multi-colored designs without the colors bleeding into one another.

For gear, such as helmets, sporting equipment, and even musical instruments, similar principles apply. However, the scale and surface texture may vary, requiring adjustments in technique. For instance, a helmet might need more detailed and smaller scale patterns compared to a large car hood. Here, artists often use finer nozzles on their airbrushes for greater detail work and reduced overspray.

In both vehicle and gear customization, finishing touches are critical. This includes the application of clear coats to protect the paint job from physical damage and UV rays, which can cause colors to fade over time. The type of clear coat can vary depending on the object and use. For example, a high-gloss finish might be preferred for a show car, while a matte finish could be better for a racing helmet to reduce glare.

Artists who specialize in custom airbrush designs on vehicles and gear often develop a signature style that can become highly sought after. As they gain experience, they might experiment with different materials and techniques, such as using metallic or pearlescent paints to create effects that change appearance under different lighting conditions.

The transition from airbrushing on flat canvases to complex, three-dimensional objects like vehicles and gear requires not only advanced airbrushing skills but also an understanding of materials and a flair for design. It's a challenging yet rewarding endeavor that allows artists to leave a personal mark on tangible, often functional items, turning ordinary objects into extraordinary pieces of art.

Using Friskets and Masks

Using friskets and masks is an advanced technique in airbrushing that allows artists to create precise, intricate designs with clean, sharp edges. This method is particularly useful for adding layers, complex patterns, and detailed foreground elements to an artwork without over-spray on other areas. Understanding how to effectively use friskets and masks can elevate the quality of a beginner's project significantly, making it an essential skill for those looking to advance their airbrushing capabilities.

A frisket is typically a thin film or a sheet of material that adheres to the surface of your project to protect certain areas from receiving paint. These are usually made from plastic or vinyl and are either self-adhesive or can be held in place with a temporary adhesive. Friskets are most beneficial when you need very sharp lines or when working on a large area where precision is crucial. They can be cut into any shape desired, making them extremely versatile for any project.

Masks, on the other hand, are similar to friskets but are often used for covering larger or more irregular areas. They can be made from various materials, including masking tape, paper, or specially designed masking fluids that can be painted on. Masks are particularly useful for protecting background areas or creating negative spaces within a design. They can be layered over each other, allowing for complex multi-colored backgrounds or intricate layered images to be created without disturbing the underlying layers.

The process of using friskets and masks involves several key steps. First, the artist must plan the layout of the artwork, deciding which areas to mask in order to achieve the desired effect. Once the areas are identified, the frisket or mask is applied to the surface. If using a frisket film, the artist will typically use a craft knife to cut out the design directly on the surface, peeling away the areas where paint is to be applied. This requires a steady hand and a keen eye for detail to ensure that the cuts are precise and do not damage the painting surface.

After applying the frisket or mask, the artist can then begin airbrushing. It's important to spray at a right angle to the surface to avoid lifting the edges of the frisket or seeping beneath the mask. This technique ensures that the paint only goes where it is intended, and the protected areas remain clean. Multiple layers of paint can be applied, each layer masked off in turn, to build up color or create shading and depth without the risk of overspray.

Once the airbrushing is complete, the friskets or masks need to be carefully removed. This should be done slowly and gently to avoid pulling up any of the underlying paint or damaging the surface. The result is a crisp, clean line or pattern that would be difficult to achieve freehand.

For beginners, mastering the use of friskets and masks can initially seem daunting due to the precision required in both application and removal. However, with practice, this technique becomes an invaluable tool in the creation of professional-looking pieces. It not only enhances the artist's ability to control the placement and intensity of color but also allows for the exploration of more complex and detailed artistic expressions. Moreover, it provides a methodical approach to creating artwork that can help beginners develop a more disciplined hand and a deeper understanding of spatial planning in visual art.

Airbrushing with Metallic and Pearlescent Paints

Airbrushing with metallic and pearlescent paints is a technique that can elevate the visual appeal of artworks by adding shimmer and depth that regular paints cannot achieve. These advanced techniques require a good understanding of the basic principles of airbrushing along with some experimentation and practice, especially for beginners transitioning to more complex projects.

Metallic and pearlescent paints differ significantly from regular airbrush paints due to their composition. Metallic paints contain tiny flakes of metal which reflect light, giving the paint its distinctive shine. Pearlescent paints, on the other hand, use mica particles to achieve a similar effect but with a pearl-like sheen that appears to change color when viewed from different angles. Both types of paints can be used to create stunning effects on a variety of surfaces including canvas, automotive exteriors, and even textiles.

The key to successful airbrushing with these types of paints lies in the preparation and application techniques. Firstly, these paints are typically thicker than standard airbrush paints due to the particles they contain. As such, they often require thinning before use. It is crucial to use the correct thinner recommended by the paint manufacturer to maintain the reflective qualities of the paint without causing clogs in the airbrush nozzle.

When applying metallic or pearlescent paints, the technique differs slightly from using regular airbrush paints. Due to the particles in the paint, maintaining a consistent distance from the surface is crucial. If the airbrush is too close to the surface, the paint may be applied too thickly, leading to a muddy appearance where the metallic or pearlescent qualities are lost. On the other hand, spraying from too far away may result in overspray where the tiny particles disperse too widely, diminishing the overall effect and wasting paint.

One effective technique is to apply these paints in several thin layers, allowing each layer to dry completely before applying the next. This builds up a smooth, even coating that maximizes the reflective properties of the paint. Between layers, it's advisable to check the work under different light sources to ensure the desired effect is being achieved and to adjust the technique if necessary.

Another consideration is the angle of application. Both metallic and pearlescent paints can look drastically different based on the angle from which they are viewed and the direction from which light hits them. Experimenting with different angles during application can help achieve a uniform luster and ensure that the effect is visible from multiple perspectives.

Cleaning the airbrush thoroughly after using metallic or pearlescent paints is more critical than with regular paints. The particles in these paints can easily settle in the airbrush mechanism and lead to clogs or damage if not cleaned properly. It's recommended to disassemble the airbrush and clean all parts individually, ensuring that no residue remains.

For beginners, practicing these techniques on scrap material or in a controlled setting can provide a valuable learning experience. Mastery of airbrushing with metallic and pearlescent paints not only broadens the range of projects one can undertake but also enhances the quality and appeal of the artworks created. With patience and practice, beginners can achieve professional-looking results that truly stand out.

Conclusion

In concluding a guide on airbrushing for beginners, it's important to reflect on the journey from the basic understanding of the equipment and techniques to the execution of complex and beautiful art pieces. Airbrushing, a versatile and dynamic form of artistic expression, offers numerous opportunities for creativity and personal growth, making it an appealing pursuit for artists of all levels.

For beginners who have embarked on this path, the progression in skill and confidence is often noticeable and gratifying. Starting with fundamental techniques such as handling the airbrush, mastering simple strokes, and understanding paint behavior, a novice can quickly find themselves delving into more intricate designs and using advanced techniques. This evolution in skill is not just about artistic growth but also about understanding how to troubleshoot common problems, maintain equipment properly, and experiment with different media and surfaces.

The versatility of airbrushing allows it to be applied across various mediums and projects. Whether creating custom automotive finishes, detailed illustrations on canvas, or delicate designs on cakes, airbrushing transcends traditional painting techniques with its ability to layer, shade, and create gradients that are smooth and visually stunning. The skills learned through airbrushing can also enhance an artist's capability in other forms of painting, offering a broader understanding of color dynamics and surface interactions.

Moreover, the community of airbrush artists is both vibrant and supportive. Newcomers find not only guidance but also inspiration from seasoned practitioners who showcase the potential of what can be achieved with an airbrush. This community is an excellent resource for continuous learning and can be a wellspring of opportunities for those looking to turn a hobby into a professional endeavor.

Finally, it's essential for beginners to remember that like any art form, airbrushing requires patience and practice. The initial challenges and learning curves are stepping stones to becoming adept in creating high-quality artworks. As beginners continue to explore and push the boundaries of what they can do with an airbrush, they not only improve their technique but also their creative vision.

In essence, starting with airbrushing opens up a world of artistic possibilities. With each project, artists can explore new techniques, blend colors in novel ways, and express ideas with a level of detail and precision that other painting methods struggle to match. Thus, airbrushing is not just a skill to be learned; it is an art form to be explored and enjoyed, offering endless opportunities for personal and artistic expression.

www.ingramcontent.com/pod-product-compliance
Lightning Source LLC
Chambersburg PA
CBHW050240230526
45470CB00005B/2035